AF352997

Colección: Libros de inglés para Infantil y Primaria

CUENTOS Y POESÍAS EN INGLÉS
PARA INFANTIL 5 AÑOS

WHAT A MESS! WHAT CAN WE DO NOW? (school)

THE LITTLE BOY CAN'T SLEEP (family)

THE TIGER STRIPES FALL DOWN (New Year and toys)

MUM, I'VE GOT A HIGH TEMPERATURE! (body and winter)

CLOTHES, CLOTHES… TOO MUCH CLOTHES (clothes)

AN ADVENTURE AT THE SUPERMARKET (food)

THE RABBITS ARE PLAYING WITH THE EASTER EGGS
(spring and Easter)

A VERY HAPPY CAT (animals)

SHARKS BY THE SEA (summer and holiday)

DINNER IS READY (Universal Children's Day)

THE GIRAFFE AND THE DALMATIAN (Halloween)

THE GOLDFISH (Peace Day)

Ninguna parte de esta publicación puede ser reproducida, almacenada o transmitida de ningún modo o medio sin la autorización previa y escrita de la autora.

Copyright © Pilar Bellés Pitarch, 2014
1ª edición: agosto 2014
ISBN de libro: 978-84-617-1334-9
Depósito Legal: CS-270-2014

Pilar Bellés Pitarch (1964) es licenciada en Filología Inglesa y profesora de inglés. Hace años que se dedica a investigar sobre las posibilidades del cuento para desarrollar la creatividad y trabajar valores. También cuenta con investigaciones sobre métodos para aprender inglés.

Estos son los cuentos y poesías que usa en sus clases de inglés. Cada cuento tiene sus imágenes en color y su poema. A los niños de esta edad les gusta recitar poemas en lengua extranjera y así, mientras escuchan el cuento en inglés interactúan y usan la lengua.

Son de gran utilidad tanto para los profesores o profesoras de inglés como para los padres y madres que quieran mejorar el nivel de inglés de sus hijos o hijas.

Pilar Bellés cuenta además con numerosas publicaciones en cuento, novela y poesía.

Publicaciones sobre cuentos plurilingües y valores en el campo de la enseñanza:

•"Telling a tale / Contemos un cuento / Contem un conte" (adaptados a los centros de interés de educación infantil).

• "Cuentos plurilingües para trabajar valores y para días especiales" (día del árbol, día de la paz, Halloween…)

•"¿Cómo hacer alumnos creativos?" (cuentos plurilingües para desarrollar la creatividad y, a la vez, trabajar valores para todas las edades).

• "No dejes que crezca sin la magia de los cuentos… según lo que quieras transmitir, elige un cuento y… cuéntaselo" (alternativa a los cuentos tradicionales).

Métodos para aprender inglés a través de la literatura:

•"Els iaios, la natura i l'amor / Los abuelos, la naturaleza y el amor / Grandparents, Love and Nature" (método de las historias plurilingües).

•"Federico y su duende / Frederick and his Goblin" (método de las historias bilingües).

Novela:

•"El diario mágico" (contra la violencia de género). Ediciones Carena.

•"Somos víctimas de una sociedad machista y cruel" (contra el machismo y la desigualdad). Ediciones Grup Lobher.

•"El mensaje" (contra el acoso y la manipulación). Ediciones Carena.

•"La rosa deshojada" (contra la violencia de género) de Pilar Bellés y Maribel Rueda. JNQ Ediciones.

•"Triunfar en tiempos difíciles" con el método de los relatos interrelacionados. JNQ Ediciones.

."Reunión de colegas" (se nos manipula sin que nos demos cuenta…). Editorial Lulu.

Biografía:
. "Toda una vida: memorias y anécdotas de Mel y Xispa". De Manuel Falcó García (Xispa) y Pilar Bellés Pitarch. Editorial viveLibro.

. Teatro: "Engaño perfecto". Editorial Lulu.

. Poesía: "Curvas en el camino". Ediciones Carena.

. Ensayo: "Educar en valores actuales a través de la literatura y otros ensayos". Editorial Lulu.

WHAT A MESS! WHAT CAN WE DO NOW?
(SCHOOL)

CHILDREN AT INFANT SCHOOL HAD GOT DIFFERENT TRAYS TO PUT PENCILS, CRAYONS, GLUES, SCISSORS, PAPERS, BOOKS, PUZZLES, PAINTS AND LATELY PLASTICINE…
ONE DAY CHILDREN WANTED TO PAINT.
'CAN WE PAINT?'
'YES, YOU CAN,' SAID THE TEACHER, 'BUT YOU MUST BE CAREFUL. DON'T PAINT ON THE TABLES.'
AFTER PAINTING, THEY CLEANED EVERYTHING.

PICK UP EVERYTHING
PENCILS, CRAYONS, GLUE,
SCISSORS, PAPERS, BOOK,
PUZZLE AND PAINTS,
BUT PLASCICINE…
NO, NO, NO.

PENCILS CRAYONS GLUE

SCISSORS PAPERS BOOK

PUZZLE PAINTS PLASTICINE

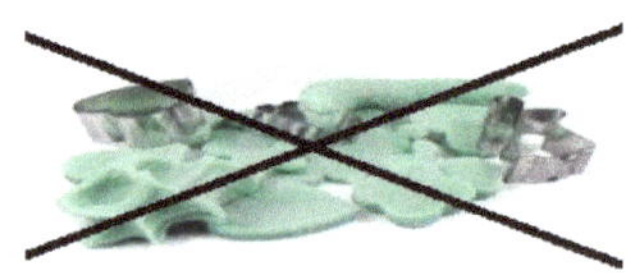

CAN WE MAKE PLASTICINE SHAPES?'
'YES, YOU CAN,' SAID THE TEACHER, 'BUT YOU MUST BE CAREFUL.'
CHILDREN MADE LOTS OF PLASTICINE SHAPES: DOGS, CATS, RABBITS, DINOSAURS… THEY HAD A NICE TIME BUT THERE WERE SMALL PLASTICINE PIECES STUCK EVERYWHERE. THE TEACHER GOT ANGRY.

WHAT A MESS!
PLASTICINE EVERYWHERE!
NO PLASTICINE, NO, NO, NO
CLEAN, CLEAN YES, YES, YES.

'WHAT A MESS! HOW AWFUL! WHAT CAN WE DO?'
'PLASTICINE MUST BE PUNISHED!' SAID ONE STUDENT.
'WE MUST CLEAN,' SAID ANOTHER STUDENT.
'OK,' SAID THE TEACHER.
ALL THE STUDENTS CLEANED THE TABLES AND PICKED UP THE SMALL PIECES OF PLASTICINE STUCK ON THE FLOOR.

WHAT A MESS!

PLASTICINE EVERYWHERE!

NO PLASTICINE, NO, NO, NO

CLEAN, YES, YES, YES.

DAYS LATER THEY COULD MAKE PLASTICINE SHAPES, BUT WHEN THEY MADE PLASTICINE SHAPES THEY MUST BE CAREFUL AND THEY MUSTN'T LEAVE SMALL PIECES STUCK ON THE FLOOR.

BE CAREFUL EVERYDAY

YOU ARE HAPPY

ONE, TWO, THREE.

WHAT A MESS!

PICK UP EVERYTHING
PENCILS, CRAYONS, GLUE,
SCISSORS, PAPERS, BOOK,
PUZZLE AND PAINTS,
BUT PLASCICINE….
NO, NO, NO.
WHAT A MESS!
PLASTICINE EVERYWHERE!
NO PLASTICINE, NO, NO, NO
CLEAN, YES, YES, YES.
BE CAREFUL EVERYDAY
YOU ARE HAPPY
ONE, TWO, THREE.

THE LITTLE BOY CAN'T SLEEP
(FAMILY)

IT WAS TIME TO TAKE A NAP. THE LITTLE BOY WANTED TO SLEEP BUT HE COULDN'T. HE WENT TO MUM AND DAD'S BEDROOM.
'CAN I STAY HERE?'
'YES, YOU CAN, BUT YOU HAVE TO SLEEP.'
THEY PLAYED AND PLAYED IN BED FOR A LONG TIME BUT THE LITTLE BOY DIDN'T SLEEP. HE WANTED TO PLAY WITH MUM AND DAD.

PLAY WITH MUM AND DAD
YES, YES, YES
SLEEP, SLEEP, SLEEP
NO, NO, NO…

THE LITTLE BOY WENT TO HIS SISTER BEDROOM.
'CAN I STAY HERE?'
'YES, YOU CAN… BUT YOU HAVE TO SLEEP.'
THE BROTHER AND HIS SISTER PLAYED TOGETHER, BUT HE COULDN'T SLEEP THERE.

STAY WITH SISTER
YES, YES, YES
PLAY, PLAY, PLAY
YES, YES, YES
SLEEP, SLEEP
NO, NO, NO

BROTHER AND SISTER

BEDROOM

THE LITTLE BOY WENT TO THE BATHROOM BUT IT WAS TOO COLD TO SLEEP. THEN HE WENT TO THE KITCHEN BUT IT WAS TOO SMALL TO SLEEP.

BATHROOM, BATHROOM
COLD, COLD, COLD
KITCHEN, KITCHEN
SMALL, SMALL, SMALL.

BATHROOM

KITCHEN

THEN HE WENT TO THE DINING ROOM BUT IT WAS TOO BIG TO SLEEP.
FINALLY THE LITTLE BOY WENT TO THE LIVING ROOM WHERE GRANNY AND GRANDDAD WERE ON THE SOFA. THEY WERE WATCHING TV.
'CAN I WATCH TV WITH YOU?'
'OK,' SAID GRANNY.
TEN MINUTES LATER HE FELL ASLEEP. FINALLY THE LITTLE BOY COULD SLEEP.

DINING ROOM
BIG, BIG, BIG
LIVING ROOM
GRANNY, GRANDDAD
LET'S HAVE FUN
SLEEP, SLEEP,
YES, YES, YES
YOU ARE HAPPY
ONE, TWO, THREE.

DINNING-ROOM

LIVING-ROOM

GRANDPARENTS

THE LITTLE BOY CAN'T SLEEP

PLAY WITH MUM AND DAD
YES, YES, YES
SLEEP, SLEEP, SLEEP
NO, NO, NO…
STAY WITH SISTER
YES, YES, YES
PLAY, PLAY, PLAY
YES, YES, YES
SLEEP, SLEEP
NO, NO, NO
BATHROOM, BATHROOM
COLD, COLD, COLD
KITCHEN, KITCHEN
SMALL, SMALL, SMALL.
DINING ROOM
BIG, BIG, BIG
LIVING ROOM
GRANNY, GRANDDAD
LET'S HAVE FUN,
SLEEP, SLEEP,
YES, YES, YES
YOU ARE HAPPY
ONE, TWO, THREE.

THE TIGER'S STRIPES FALL DOWN
(NEW YEAR AND TOYS)

ONCE UPON A TIME THERE WAS A BIG TIGER THAT HAD LOTS OF TOYS: A CAR, A BALL, A DRUM, A KITE, A BALLOON, A TRAIN, A BOAT, A TEDDY BEAR…

THE TIGER HAS GOT
A CAR, A BALL, A DRUM,
A PARKING, A KITE AND A DRUM
A KITE, A BALLOON, A TRAIN,
A BOAT AND TEDDY BEAR.

CAR   BALL   DRUM

KITE   BALLOON   TRAIN

BOAT   TEDDY BEAR

HE WAS WALKING HAPPILY ACROSS THE
JUNGLE AND HE HEARD A TERRIBLE NOISE.
"BANG"
'WHAT'S THAT ON THE FLOOR? IS IT MY
STRIPE? OH NO! IT'S OK… LET'S GO!'

BANG, BANG
ONE STRIPE OUT
OH NO!
LET'S GO…

ONE MINUTE LATER…
"BANG!"
'ANOTHER STRIPE OUT! I'VE GOT LOTS OF STRIPES… LET'S GO!'
ONE MINUTE LATER…
"BANG!"
'THAT'S ENOUGH!'

ONE STRIPE OUT
OH NO!
LET'S GO…
THAT'S ENOUGH!

'WHAT'S THAT?
LOOK UP, IN THE TREE!' SAID SOMEONE.
'THAT'S ENOUGH!' SAID HE.
A MONKEY WAS THROWING STREAMERS AND
SAYING THESE WORDS:
'MERRY CHRISTMAS AND HAPPY NEW YEAR!'
 'MERRY CHRISTMAS AND HAPPY NEW YEAR!'
REPEATED THE TIGER AND HE SMILED.

WHAT'S THAT?
LOOK AT THE TREE
HAPPY NEW YEAR
HAPPY NEW YEAR
FOR YOU AND ME.

HAPPY NEW YEAR

THE TIGER HAS GOT
A LORRY, A CAR, AND A BALL,
A PARKING, A KITE AND A DRUM
A TRAIN, A BOAT AND A BALLOON,
AND A TEDDY BEAR.
BANG, BANG
ONE STRIPE OUT
OH NO!
LET'S GO…
THAT'S ENOUGH!
WHAT'S THAT?
LOOK AT THE TREE
HAPPY NEW YEAR
HAPPY NEW YEAR
FOR YOU AND ME.

MUM, I'VE GOT A HIGHT TEMPERATURE!
(BODY AND WINTER)

THE SMALL MARIA HAD GOT A HIGH TEMPERA-
TURE WHEN SHE CAME BACK FROM SCHOOL.
'WHAT'S THE MATTER?' ASKED MUM.
'I'M AWFUL! I'M HOT! IT'S FOGGY. I CAN'T SEE,
MYEYES HURT, MY TUMMY HURTS, MY HEAD
HURTS, MY MOUTH HURTS, MY NOSE HURTS,
MY HAND HURTS, MY LEGS HURT…'
SIT DOWN,' SAID MUM, 'LET'S PUT THE
THERMOMETER IN YOUR MOUTH.'
'YOU MUST HAVE THIS MEDICINE.'

I'M HOT, I'M HOT
OH NO! OH NO!
IT'S MY HEAD
AND MY BODY,
AND MY LEGS…

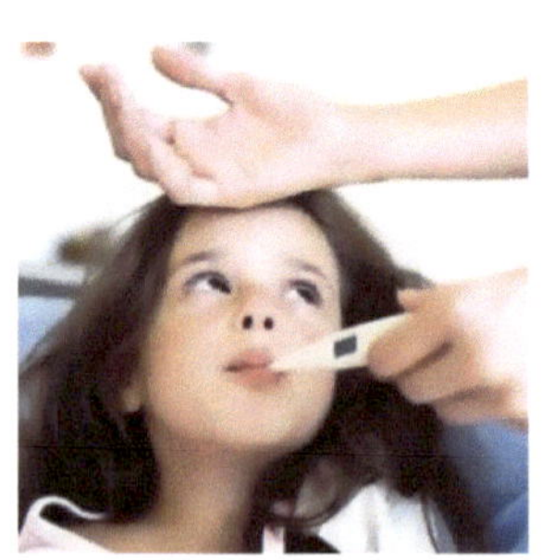

MARIA AND HER MOTHER PLAYED THE GAME: "WALKING IN A FOGGY DAY". MARIA CLOSED HER EYES AND MUM GUIDED HER TO THE SHOWER.
'CLOSE YOUR EYES. IT'S HOT. LET'S GO TO THE RAIN. IT'S RAINING'

CLOSE YOUR EYES
WALK, WALK, WALK
LET'S GO TO THE RAIN
YES, YES, YES…
MEDICINE, MEDICINE
YES, YES, YES.

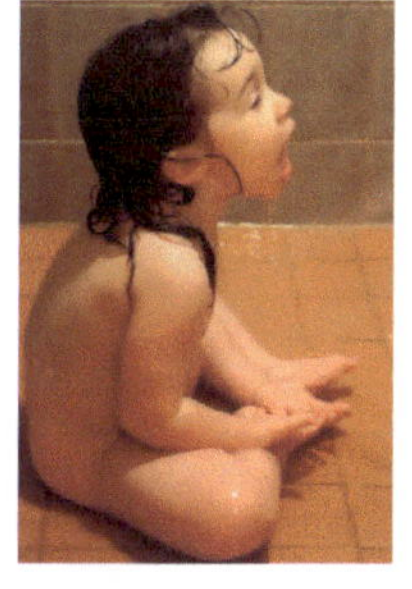

AFTER HAVING A SHOWER AND SOME MEDICINE MARIA GOT BETTER.
'LET'S PUT THE THERMOMETER IN YOUR MOUTH.'
'YOU ARE NOT HOT…YOU ARE HEALTHY. AND I'M VERY HAPPY.'
'I LOVE YOU, MUM. THANK YOU'

I'M NOT HOT
NO, NO, NO
THANK YOU MUM
I'M OK
WE ARE HAPPY
ONE, TWO, THREE.

I'M HOT

I'M HOT, I'M HOT
OH NO! OH NO!
IT'S MY HEAD
AND MY BODY,
AND MY LEGS…

CLOSE YOUR EYES

WALK, WALK, WALK

LET'S GO TO THE RAIN

YES, YES, YES…

MEDICINE, MEDICINE

YES, YES, YES

I'M NOT HOT

NO, NO, NO

THANK YOU MUM

I'M OK

WE ARE HAPPY

ONE, TWO, THREE.

CLOTHES, CLOTHES, TOO MUCH CLOTHES....
(CLOTHES)

MUM LIKED SHOPPING. SHE WENT SHOPPING WITH HER CHILDREN. EVERYTHING IS CHEAPER. SHE WANTED TO BUY EVERYTHING.

MUM, BROTHER, SISTER,
GO SHOPPING
THEY ARE HAPPY
ONE, TWO, THREE.

FIRST THE BROTHER:
'DO YOU WANT A JACKET?' SAID MUM.
'NO, I DON'T. I'VE GOT LOTS OF JACKETS,' SAID THE
BROTHER.
'DO YOU WANT TROUSERS?' SAID MUM.
'NO, I DON'T.'
'WHAT ABOUT THESE SHOES?'
'I DON'T LIKE THIS COLOUR.'
MUM TRIED TO BUY EVERYTHING BUT HER SON DIDN'T WANT TO BUY IT.

A JACKET, A JACKET,
NO, NO, NO…
TROUSERS, TROUSERS,
NO, NO, NO…
SHOES, SHOES,
NO, NO, NO…

BUT THE SISTER LIKED SHOPPING AND CLOTHES.
'DO YOU WANT A SKIRT?' SAID MUM.
'YES, I DO,' SAID SHE. 'CAN I CHOOSE IT?'
'IT ALL DEPENDS…'
'DO YOU LIKE THIS SHIRT?'
'YES, I DO. CAN I TRY IT?'
'OK.'
'AND I WANT A NEW PYJAMA, MUM.'

I WANT A SKIRT,
YES, YES, YES
I WANT A SHIRT,
YES, YES, YES
I WANT A PYJAMA
YES, YES, YES.

SKIRT

SHIRT

PYJAMA

GIRL

THEY BOUGHT CLOTHES, TOO MUCH CLOTHES.
'LET'S PAY.'
THEN MUM SAW THE TICKET.
'IT'S AWFUL! WHAT DID YOU BUY? IT'S TOO EXPENSIVE. WE EXCEEDED OUR LIMITS. NEXT DAY WE'LL STAY AT HOME.'

LET'S PAY, LET'S PAY
OK, OK, OK
WHAT'S THAT?
OH NO! OH NO!
CLOTHES, CLOTHES,
NO, NO, NO
STAY AT HOME
YES, YES, YES
WE ARE HAPPY
ONE, TWO, THREE.

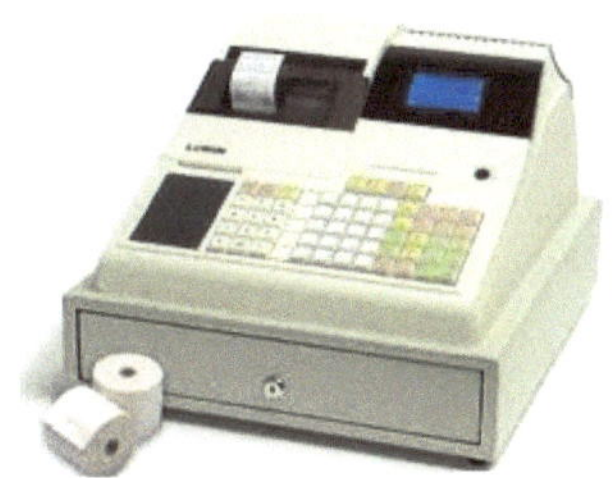

CLOTHES, CLOTHES

MUM, BROTHER, SISTER,
GO SHOPPING
THEY ARE HAPPY
ONE, TWO, THREE.

A JACKET, A JACKET,
NO, NO, NO…
TROUSERS, TROUSERS,
NO, NO, NO…
SHOES, SHOES,
NO, NO, NO…

I WANT A SKIRT,
YES, YES, YES…
I WANT A SHIRT,
YES, YES, YES…
I WANT A PYJAMA
YES, YES, YES…

LET'S PAY, LET'S PAY
OK, OK, OK
WHAT'S THAT?
OH NO! OH NO!

CLOTHES, CLOTHES,
NO, NO, NO
STAY AT HOME
YES, YES, YES
WE ARE HAPPY
ONE, TWO, THREE.

AN ADVENTURE AT THE SUPERMARKET
(FOOD)

MUM WENT SHOPPING TO THE SUPERMARKET.
GRANNY AND MARIA WENT WITH HER.
'LET'S GO TO THE TOYS SECTION' SAID MARIA VERY
EXCITED.
'NO TOYS HERE,' SAID MUM.
'CAN I GET INTO THE TROLLEY?'
'YES, ALL RIGHT,' SAID MUM.

MUM, MARIA AND GRANNY
WENT TO THE SUPERMARKET,
TOYS, TOYS, TOYS
NO, NO, NO.
TROLLEY, TROLLEY, TROLLEY,
YES, YES, YES…

GRANNY, SISTER AND MUM   TOYS

THEY WENT TO THE GREENGROCER'S TO GET
BANANAS, ORANGES, APPLES AND
VEGETABLES.
THEN THEY GOT MILK, MEAT, AND FISH TOO.

BANANAS, ORANGES,
APPLES VEGETABLES,
MILK AND MEAT.

BANANAS   ORANGES

APPLES   VEGETABLES

MILK   MEAT   FISH

THE TROLLEY WAS FULL OF FOOD AND MARIA
HAD TO GO OUT.
SUDDENLY SHE FOUND A SMALL TOY, A CAR
TOY FROM A SANDWICH BAR, ON THE FLOOR.
'A CAR, IT'S FOR ME? I'M HAPPY!' SHE SMILED.

WHAT'S THAT?
IT'S A TOY CAR.
IS IT FOR ME?
OH! WOW!

LET'S PAY,' SAID MUM.
THEN THEY SAW A LITTLE BOY CRYING.
MARIA LOOKED AT HIM:
'WHAT'S THE MATTER?'
'MY TOY CAR IS LOST!'
MARIA GAVE HIM THE TOY CAR.
'HERE YOU ARE!,' SAID MARIA.
'OH, THANK YOU!,' SAID THE BOY. 'LET'S PLAY TOGETHER!'
'YES.'

HERE YOU ARE!
THANK YOU!
LET'S PLAY TOGETHER…
YES, YES, YES.

EVERYONE WAS HAPPY.
'I'M PROUD OF YOU, MY SWEET,' SAID MUM.
'WHAT ABOUT BURGER?,' SAID GRANNY.
'HURRAY!' SAID MARIA.
MARIA HAD A TOY CAR WITH HER BURGER.
MARIA SMILED. IT WAS A GREAT ADVENTURE
AT THE SUPER-MARKET.

LET'S HAVE DINNER
YES, YES, YES
A BURGER AND A TOY CAR
YES, YES, YES,
WE ARE HAPPY
ONE, TWO, THREE.

FOOD

MUM, MARIA AND GRANNY
WENT TO THE SUPERMARKET,
TOYS, TOYS, TOYS
NO, NO, NO.
TROLLEY, TROLLEY, TROLLEY,
YES, YES, YES…
BANANAS, ORANGES, APPLES
VEGETABLES, MILK AND MEAT.
WHAT'S THAT?
IT'S A TOY CAR.
IS IT FOR ME?
OH! WOW!
HERE YOU ARE!
THANK YOU!
LET'S PLAY TOGETHER…
YES, YES, YES.
LET'S HAVE DINNER
YES, YES, YES
A BURGER AND A TOY CAR
YES, YES, YES,
WE ARE HAPPY
ONE, TWO, THREE.

THE RABBITS ARE PLAYING WITH EASTER EGGS

(SPRING AND EASTER)

IT WAS EASTER DAY. CHILDREN WERE PLAYING IN THE GARDEN. MUM AND DAD WERE WATCHING THEM.
THE BROTHER, HIS SISTER AND THEIR FRIENDS WERE LOOKING FOR EASTER EGGS. THERE WERE EASTER EGGS HIDDEN IN THE GARDEN.

IT'S EASTER TIME

CHILDREN IN THE GARDEN

LOOK FOR EASTER EGGS.
HIDDEN, HIDDEN, HIDDEN

'HOW MANY EASTER EGGS HAVE YOU FOUND?'
ASKED MUM.
'I'VE FOUND ONE EGG?' SAID THE SISTER.
'TWO EGGS,' SAID THE BROTHER.
'I DIDN'T FIND ANY EGG,' SAID ONE FRIEND.
'NOR DID I,' SAID ANOTHER FRIEND, 'THERE ARE NO
EGGS IN THE GARDEN.'

THERE ARE THREE EGGS
THERE ARE TWO EGGS
THERE'S ONE EGG
THERE ARE NO EGGS…
WHERE ARE THE EASTER EGGS?

WHERE ARE THE EASTER EGGS?' ASKED MUM.
'I DON'T KNOW' SAID DAD.
'DON'T ASK ME!' SAID GRANNY.
"CAN THEY FIND ANY EGG?." "OH NO!"
THE BROTHER FOUND SOMETHING:
'DAD, MUM, HERE IS A RABBIT DEN.'
'LET'S SEE…'
THERE WAS A FAMILY OF RABBITS PLAYING WITH THE EASTER EGGS.
'OH DEAR!' SAID THE BROTHER.
'THEY ARE NICE. I LIKE THEM,' SAID THE SISTER.

WHERE ARE THE EASTER EGGS?
RABBITS, RABBITS
ARE PLAYING WITH EASTER EGGS,
GOOD BYE RABBITS
GOOD BYE, GOOD BYE.

'LET'S GO TO HAVE LUNCH,' SAID MUM.
'RABBITS CAN PLAY WITH THE EASTER EGGS…
HAPPY EASTER!'
'HAPPY EASTER!' REPEATED ALL THE FAMILY.
"HAPPY EASTER, RABBITS!"

GOOD BYE RABBITS
GOOD BYE, GOOD BYE
HAPPY EASTER, HAPPY EASTER
HAPPY EASTER EVERYONE.

EASTER EGGS

IT'S EASTER TIME
CHILDREN IN THE GARDEN
LOOK FOR EASTER EGGS.
HIDDEN, HIDDEN, HIDDEN.
THERE ARE THREE EGGS
THERE ARE TWO EGGS
THERE'S ONE EGG
THERE ARE NO EGGS…
WHERE ARE THE EASTER EGGS?
RABBITS, RABBITS
ARE PLAYING WITH EASTER EGGS,
GOOD BYE RABBITS
GOOD BYE, GOOD BYE
HAPPY EASTER, HAPPY EASTER
HAPPY EASTER EVERYONE.

A VERY HAPPY CAT
(ANIMALS)

IT WAS BREAKFAST TIME. THE CAT DOES HIS
HOMEWORK EVERY DAY. HE LIKES CAT FOOD.
MUM HAD GIVEN HIM A LOT OF CAT FOOD.
A MOUTH IS WATCHING HIM:
'SOME FOOT, PLEASE?'
'NO, NO, NO. YOU MUST DO YOUR HOME-WORK.
'OK,' SAID THE MOUSE AND HE WENT AWAY.

DO YOUR HOMEWORK
YES, YES, YES,
CAT FOOD, CAT FOOD,
YES, YES, YES.

AN ENORMOUS DOG ARRIVED. THE DOG WANTED THE FOOD. THE CAT IS SCARED".
'GIVE ME THE FOOD OR I'LL BITE YOU.'
"WHAT A PROBLEM!"
THE CAT HAD GOT AN IDEA. HE CALLED THE MOUSE:
'MOUSE! FOOD! FOOD! YOU CAN EAT THE FOOD!'

FOOD, PLEASE?
NO, NO, NO…
GIVE ME THE FOOD,
OH, OH, OH!
MOUSE, MOUSE
FOOD, FOOD, FOOD.

WHEN THE DOG SAW THE MOUSE HE GOT ANGRY. THE MOUSE ESCAPED. THE DOG CHASED AND CHASED THE MOUSE. HE WANTED THE FOOD.
SO, THE CAT ATE HAPPILY HIS FOOD.
'YOU ARE VERY NAUGHTY,' SAID THE MOUSE.
MEANWHILE THE CAT ATE HAPPILY.
'DO YOUR HOMEWORK AND BE HAPPY,' SAID THE CAT.

MOUSE RUNS, RUNS,

CAT EATS, EATS,

HAPPY, HAPPY,

ONE, TWO, THREE.

DO YOUR HOMEWORK!

DO YOUR HOMEWORK
YES, YES, YES,
CAT FOOD, CAT FOOD,
YES, YES, YES.
FOOD, PLEASE?
NO, NO, NO…
GIVE ME THE FOOD,
OH, OH, OH!
MOUSE, MOUSE
FOOD, FOOD, FOOD.
DOG RUNS, RUNS,
MOUSE RUNS, RUNS,
CAT EATS, EATS,
HE IS HAPPY, HAPPY,
ONE, TWO, THREE.

SHARKS BY THE SEA!
(SUMMER AND HOLIDAY)

EACH MORNING MUM, DAD AND BROTHER TOOK HER DOG FOR A WALK TO THE SEASIDE. THEY SAW SOMETHING BLACK IN THE WAVES. 'WHAT'S THAT?' ASKED THE SMALLEST BROTHER. 'IS IT A SHARK?'
'NO, IT ISN'T,' ANSWERED MUM. 'THERE ARE NOT SHARKS THERE.'

WHAT'S THAT?
BLACK, BLACK, BLACK.
A SHARK, A SHARK,
GREY, GREY, GREY
NO, NO, NO…

IS IT A WHALE?'
'NO, IT ISN'T. IT'S TOO SMALL TO BE A WHALE.'
'IS IT A STARFISH?'
'NO, IT ISN'T ORANGE.'

A WHALE, A WHALE,
BLACK AND GREY
NO, NO, NO…
A STARFISH, A STARFISH,
ORANGE, ORANGE,
NO, NO, NO…

THEY SIT ON A ROCK TO WATCH. THE DOG BARKED, "BOW-BOW!"
'WHAT'S THAT?
THEY TOUCHED IT WITH A LONG STICK. IT WAS A MESSAGE IN A BOTTLE. IT SAYS: "HAPPY HOLIDAY"

A MESSAGE IN A BOTTLE,
YES, YES, YES,
HAPPY HOLIDAY
ONE, TWO, THREE.

HAPPY HOLIDAY

SHARK
WHALE
STARFISH
FISH
SEAHORSE
CRAB

WHAT'S THAT?

WHAT'S THAT?
BLACK , BLACK, BLACK.
A SHARK, A SHARK,
GREY, GREY, GREY
NO, NO, NO…
A WHALE, A WHALE,
BLACK AND GREY
NO, NO, NO…
A STARFISH, A STARFISH,
ORANGE, ORANGE,
NO, NO, NO…
A MESSAGE IN A BOTTLE,
YES, YES, YES,
HAPPY HOLIDAY
ONE, TWO, THREE.

DINNER IS READY
(UNIVERSAL CHILDREN'S DAY)

ONCE UPON A TIME THERE WAS A CHILD AND HIS FAMILY. HE PLAYS ON HIS CARPET. HE TAKES OUT HIS TOYS TO PLAY. THEN HE MUST PUT THEM IN.

'SWEET, THE TOYS,' SAYS MUM.

'JUST A MINUTE…'

'JUST…NOW!'

MUM IS SERIOUS. HE PUTS HIS TOYS IN HIS TOY
BOX.

TOYS, TOYS, TOYS,
PICK UP YOUR TOYS.

'DINNER'S READY!' SAYS MUM.
THE CHILD USUALLY WASHES HIS HANDS, HE PUTS ON HIS BIB AND HE RUNS TO THE TABLE. HE EATS RICE WITH PRAWNS. HE WATCHES CARTOONS AND, FINALLY HE FALLS ASLEEP IN HIS BLANKET.

HANDS, HANDS, HANDS,
WASH YOUR HANDS.
FOOD, FOOD, FOOD,
EAT YOUR FOOD,
NAP, NAP, NAP,
TAKE A NAP,

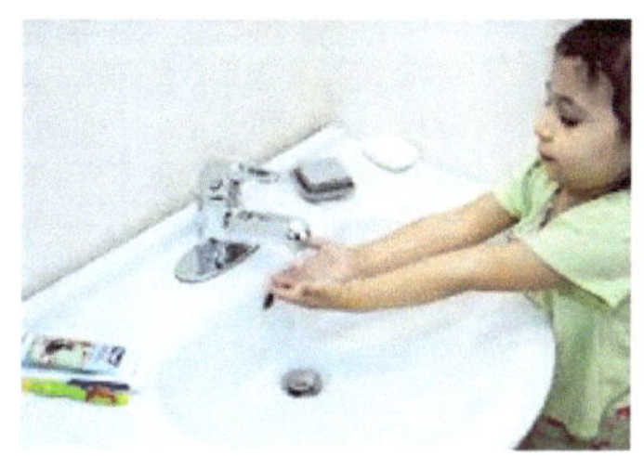

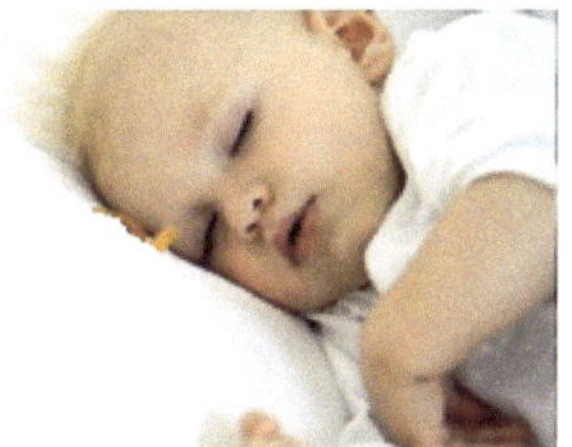

THIS DAY THERE IS DIFFERENT FOOD: LENTIL SOUP.
'MUM, MY RICE IS BLACK. IT'S BURNT UP.'
'IT'S LENTIL SOUP.'
'I DON'T WANT IT. I WANT MY RICE WITH PRAWNS!'

LENTILS, LENTILS, LENTILS,
NO, NO, NO,
RICE WITH PRAWNS
YES, YES, YES,

'NO! I GO TO WATCH CARTOONS AND TO TAKE A NAP.'
THAT DAY THE VIDEO IS DISCONNECTED AND HIS
BLANKET IS NOT THERE.

DVD, DVD, DVD,
NO, NO, NO,
TELEVISION, TELEVISION,
NO, NO, NO,
NAP, NAP, NAP,
NO, NO, NO.

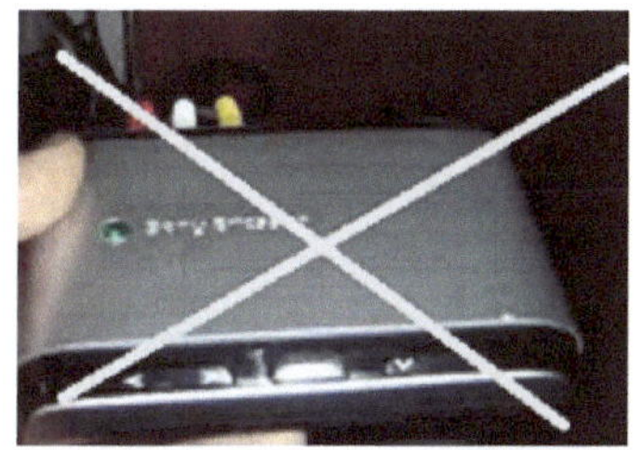

'WHAT'S THE MATTER, MUM?
'CHILDREN THAT EAT EVERYTHING HAVE VIDEO AND SIESTA. THEY ARE HEALTHY AND STRONG. BUT CHILDREN THAT DON'T EAT THEIR FOOD HAVE SERIOUS PROBLEMS.
'OK. ONLY A SPOONFUL.'
THE CHILD EATS A SPOONFUL AND THEN ANOTHER. HE EATS LENTIL SOUP. HE EATS TWO BOWLS OF LENTILS.
LITTLE BY LITTLE THE CHILD EATS EVERYTHING.

EAT EVERYTHING,
YES, YES, YES…
YOU ARE HAPPY,
ONE, TWO, THREE.

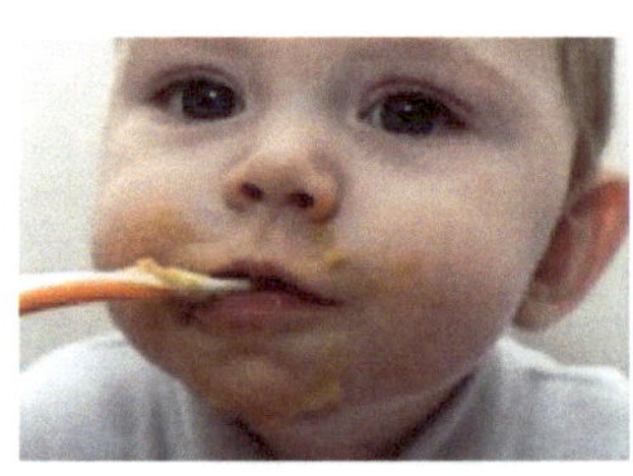

FAMILY

TOYS, TOYS, TOYS,
PICK UP YOUR TOYS.
HANDS, HANDS, HANDS,
WASH YOUR HANDS.
FOOD, FOOD, FOOD,
EAT YOUR FOOD,
NAP, NAP, NAP,
TAKE A NAP,
LENTILS, LENTILS, LENTILS,
NO, NO, NO,
RICE WITH PRAWNS
YES, YES, YES,
DVD, DVD, DVD,
NO, NO, NO,
TELEVISION, TELEVISION,
NO, NO, NO,
NAP, NAP, NAP,
NO, NO, NO.
EAT EVERYTHING,
YES, YES, YES…
YOU ARE HAPPY,
ONE, TWO, THREE.

THE GIRAFFE AND THE DALMATIAN
(HALLOWEEN)

ONCE UPON A TIME THERE WAS A PLACE IN THE FOREST WHERE ONLY GIRAFFES LIVED. THEY HAD GOT
EVERYTHING THAT THEY WANTED: FOOD, PEACE,
FAMILY… BUT THE SMALLER GIRAFFE COULDN'T PLAY.
IT IS HALLOWEEN. THE SMALLER GIRAFFE GOES OUT
OF THE FOREST TO LOOK FOR CHILDREN TO PLAY WITH AND TO CELEBRATE HALLOWEEN. SHE GOES TO A FARM AND SHE FINDS A DALMATIAN PUPPY.

GIRAFFE, GIRAFFE,
SAD, SAD, SAD.
DALMATIAN, DALMATIAN,
SAD, SAD, SAD.

'WHAT A STRANGE DOG!' WHISPERS THE DALMATIAN.
'WHAT A STRANGE GIRAFFE! IT HASN'T GOT A LONG NECK!' SAYS SHE.
'YOU CAN'T GO ONTO MY FARM, YOUR NECK IS TOO LONG,' SAYS THE DALMATIAN.
'OH! DO YOU LIVE ON A FARM?' SAYS THE GIRAFFE.
'THEN, YOU AREN'T A GIRAFFE.
'NO, NO, NO. I'M A DALMATIAN. I LIVE ON A FARM WITH DOGS AND PIGS. I HAVEN'T SEEN OTHER ANIMALS. I'M AFRAID TO GO OUT OF THE FARM.'
'YES, IT'S ALWAYS THE SAME, ALTHOUGH I WOULD
LIKE TO VISIT YOUR FARM AND CELEBRATE HALLOWEEN.'

PLAY, PLAY, PLAY
YES, YES, YES.
CELEBRATE HALLOWEEN
YES, YES, YES

THE NEXT DAY THE DALMATIAN INVITES THE GIRAFFE TO THE FARM. THE GIRAFFE LIKES IT. THEY CELEBRATE HALLOWEEN WITH THE OTHER ANIMALS OF THE FARM.
THE GIRAFFE DISGUISES HERSELF AS A WITCH AND
THE DALMATIAN DISGUISES HIMSELF AS A GHOST.
THEY GET A LOT OF SWEETS.

SWEETS, SWEETS,
YES, YES, YES.
FRIENDS, FRIENDS,
YES, YES, YES.

IT DOESN'T MEAN THE DIFFERENCES BETWEEN THEM. THEY ARE HAPPY BECAUSE THEY PLAY TOGETHER.
AND THEY LIVED HAPPILY EVER AFTER.

PLAY WITH FRIENDS
YES, YES, YES.
THEY ARE HAPPY
ONE, TWO, THREE.

FRIENDS

GIRAFFE, GIRAFFE,
SAD, SAD, SAD.
DALMATIAN, DALMATIAN,
SAD, SAD, SAD.
PLAY, PLAY, PLAY
YES, YES, YES.
CELEBRATE HALLOWEEN
YES, YES, YES.
SWEETS, SWEETS,
YES, YES, YES.
FRIENDS, FRIENDS,
YES, YES, YES.
PLAY WITH FRIENDS
YES, YES, YES.
THEY ARE HAPPY
ONE, TWO, THREE.

THE GOLDFISH
(*PEACE DAY)*

ONCE UPON A TIME THERE WAS A BLUE, ORANGE AND GREEN GOLDFISH. HE IS VERY NICE LOOKING. HE SWIMS OUT TO SEA AND MOVES HIS TAIL WHEN HE IS NEXT TO ANOTHER LESS NICE-LOOKING FISH. HE CONSIDERS HIMSELF THE PRETTIEST IN THE WORD. HE DOESN'T TALK TO ANYBODY BECAUSE HE THINKS HE IS THE BEST IN THE WORLD. ONE DAY THE GOLDFISH IS SWIMMING AND A CRAB PULLS ON HIS TAIL.
'LEAVE ME ALONE!' SAYS THE GOLDFISH.

GOLDFISH, GOLDFISH
BLUE, ORANGE AND GREEN,
FISH, FISH, FISH
SWIM, SWIM, SWIM.

HE GOES ON SWIMMING IN THE SEA. WHEN HE COMES BACK THE CRAB PULLS ON HIS TAIL AGAIN.
'DON'T DISTURB ME OR I'LL STRIKE YOU.'
HE GOES ON SWIMMING. WHEN HE COMES BACK THE CRAB TOUCHES HIS TAIL AGAIN. THE GOLDFISH IS FURIOUS. HE WANTS TO STRIKE THE CRAB. HE SEES THE CRAB IS SCARED.
'I JUST WANT TO PLAY,' SAYS THE CRAB.
'WHAT?' SAYS THE GOLDFISH. 'WHAT KIND OF GAME?'
'WHAT ABOUT BULLS?'

CRAB, CRAB, CRAB,
PULL, PULL, PULL.
SWIM, SWIM, SWIM,
PULL, PULL, PULL.
ANGRY, ANGRY, ANGRY,
SCARED, SCARED, SCARED.
PLAY, PLAY, PLAY,
YES, YES, YES.

THEY PLAY. THE CRAB IS THE BULL AND THE GOLDFISH, THE BULLFIGHTER. THEY HAVE FUN TOGETHER.
AFTER THAT THE CRAB LOOKS FOR THE GOLDFISH TO PLAY EVERY DAY.
NOW THE GOLDFISH ISN'T SELFISH. HE HAS GOT A FRIEND AND HE IS HAPPY PLAYING WITH IT.

FRIENDS, FRIENDS, FRIENDS,
YES, YES, YES.
SELFISH, SELFISH, SELFISH,
NO, NO, NO.
HAPPY, HAPPY, HAPPY,
YES, YES, YES.
HAPPY PEACE DAY
ONE, TWO, THREE.

THE GOLDFISH

GOLDFISH, GOLDFISH
BLUE, ORANGE AND GREEN,
FISH, FISH, FISH
SWIM, SWIM, SWIM.
CRAB, CRAB, CRAB,
PULL, PULL, PULL.
SWIM, SWIM, SWIM,
PULL, PULL, PULL.
ANGRY, ANGRY, ANGRY,
SCARED, SCARED, SCARED.
PLAY, PLAY, PLAY,
YES, YES, YES.
FRIENDS, FRIENDS, FRIENDS,
YES, YES, YES.
SELFISH, SELFISH, SELFISH,
NO, NO, NO.
HAPPY, HAPPY, HAPPY,
YES, YES, YES.
HAPPY PEACE DAY
ONE, TWO, THREE.

www.ingramcontent.com/pod-product-compliance
Lightning Source LLC
LaVergne TN
LVHW051454180726
843512LV00001B/30

Let's Begin!

Phalak Betab

Story 1

Was I Supposed To Be Happy Or Sad?

"I was supposed to reach home with my father as it was my marriage two weeks ahead. I was too excited like any other bride-to-be; after I was getting hitched to the love of my life. But, I had never imagined that my father's coffin would accompany me" murmured Shenali Singh who has made peace with the fact that life and death are bound to happen anytime, anywhere.

"I didn't get any morning text from my father like all other days. I checked social media and there I came across some random person who was trying to contact me. I made the most horrifying call and the voice told me the bitter truth. He was no more!"

"He was putting up at a location little far from where I was residing. I didn't tell my mother and 2 sisters whom I knew were emotionally weak. I had no option than to act stronger. I made my move towards him and there I was standing looking at his face. He was lying motionless, I was stunned…and he eventually accompanied me back home"

"I wanted him to see me as a bride; I wanted him to cry on my 'Doli' just the way he did during my sister's marriage. I got married 2 weeks ahead in a much simpler manner than he would have imagined. All the bookings were canceled; we decided to get married within the boundary of our house. Was I supposed to be happy or sad? I didn't know but I had to be strong and rigid. I have not cried in front of my mother till date! I didn't cry at my doli too! My husband and his family have always been the biggest supporters and strength for me. In a family which had 4 females and 1 male, we had lost 1 male but there we were welcoming another male. I cursed myself for my father's death, I lost faith in God".

"Gradually things changed, my marriage helped me to overcome the pain. When everyone else refused to open the coffin, my husband did that! No one can ever replace my father but at least I have someone who can share that pain with me. I miss my daddy each moment!" Shenali Singh.

Story 2

Are You Albe To Rdea Tihs Corrcelty?

Ishant is twinned with Nishant and they both are dyslexic. Dyslexia is a learning disorder which restricts a basic flow in writing, reading, speaking, and understanding. This is exactly what we say in the film Taare Zameen Par which portrayed the life of a dyslexic boy?

"Ever since I was a child, I found reading very stressful so I would always avoid it. I was not even good with grades in my school days. Soon, I figured out that I and my twin brother is dyslexic. We would have to struggle to read each word and thus we could never read beyond 2 continuous pages. Gradually we developed a keen interest in Technology related to virtual and mixed reality. YouTube and videos were the only sources of knowledge for us. Progressively, we started reading texts about this particular technology on the internet and books. But, we take swift halts when we read. It usually involves black coffee and online gaming." said Ishant in a stammered yet confident tone."

"Even though we can't read at a stretch, we can read any length of text if that is related to our topic of interest which is of course technology. We were always afraid of our father and thus we never touched his computer till the time we took admission in engineering and realized the fact that science is beautiful. Today we have developed software for Microsoft product which has the potential to revolutionize the learning process. We never knew we could do this." added Nishant in a stammered yet confident tone.

You would have read the heading of this text easily but Nishant, Ishant find it difficult. They say that they have to read each word individually.

After meeting Ishant, Nishant I googled 'Dyslexia' and found out that this disorder has no connection to the intelligence of a person.

Story 3

When Relationships Weigh Higher!

"I was the Regional Manager of a renowned Pharmaceutical Company and was earning far more than me and my family desired but I chose to quit my job to spend some quality time with my children and wife. I think relationships play higher value than any amount of salary" says 40 years old Vikas Madahar who is a living example of selflessness.

"I was too indulged with my high-salaried job that I completely forgot my true responsibilities towards my family. Earning money is surely important but that should never be at the cost of detachment in relationships. I have saved enough money for my 2 daughter's wedding. There is no stoppage to desires but I have understood that if you mark a full stop to your fantasies, the whole world seems much attractive. I and my daughters are just like friends, we often go for picnics. I feel proud of myself when I see pleased smile on their faces. My wife earns better than me now and it is again a matter of pride for me" he added.

Story 4

When You Fuel Your Passion!

"One picture out of focus is a mistake, ten pictures out of focus is experimentation, and one hundred pictures out of focus is a style. I picked up a camera for the first time just to click my Dog's picture. Soon I discovered that time, people, beauty, nature and everything around us has a story behind them. Thus, all my clicks would have something to share; something that people were missing out in their lives.

My pictures embraced nature and humanity. The most beautiful thing in this world is to admire the creation of God and I am glad that I not only admire it but Capture it forever" says Nitin Rai Chaudhary, a passionate photographer who started his career with just 47 bucks in his pocket but revolutionary ideas in his mind.

"It is not about the camera, it's something beyond it. It depends on the way you observe and see things. It's about the EYE and I think you don't need a degree to be a renowned photographer because you can't see gratitude, purity and peace in things with a degree" added Nitin who now owns a Digital Company. His passion crafted ways for him as he trusted his caliber. Hope each one of us gets the courage to Trust our instincts!

Story 5

When You Follow Your Passion, You Enlighten Yourself!

Flashback….. When she was 5, she was seen using crayons. When she turned 10, she would often draw cards for her friends/family. When she turned 15, she would still paint her imagination!

Present – She is in her 20's and her life is filled with colors. She never left her passion! "Art is so alluring that once you get into it, you get so much involved that time passes by in a jiffy. I always wanted to follow my passion to comprehend real happiness. I had the option to pursue a job and earn well but I dared to follow the ultimate bliss. It's been 3 years that I have been learning sketching and oil painting professionally. I realize that the current era demands an artist to showcase their skills on social media sites to gain appreciation and recognition. Else, you miss the bus. I am planning to take my skills to that platform now" Ashmita Sodhi, an Artist. "All parents shower love and blessings on their children. My parents are no different apart from the fact that they understood that to be blessed is to be an awakened soul and Art can act as a mediator for that".

Phalak Betab

Story 6

Isn't He An Inspiration For Youngsters Facing Troubles With Their Lives?

"I was a 12th Grader when my father passed away. I, my mother and my younger brother were left empty-handed. All those folly people never support you at the time of distress. I was the son of a senior fire consultant and there was no way I could have let my father down. I kept my confidence alive and fire burning with a mission to provide a smooth lifestyle to my family."

"Without any degree in my hand, I joined a Toy company (Hamleys) as a fun consultant. Customers would often mock at me due to my poor conversation skills and inability to respond swiftly. Those were the best days of my life; I learned spoken skills, vocabulary and vast knowledge about the Retail sector.

I kept the passion mobile and it took me not more than a year to completely understand the professional aspects of this sector" says Gurleen Singh who is just 21 and has now joined Charles & Keith as a

Senior Sales Executive. He is currently pursuing his MBA from distance education.

Story 7

Stepping Out Of Rat Race!

"I secured 96% marks in my 10th grade. It was certain for everyone around that I would choose Non-medical or Medical as core subjects. I believe that scoring good grades must not be coupled with science directly. It is a mere misconception. I have opted for ARTS. Many were disappointed with me but I know it takes courage to step out of rat race. My aim is to become an IAS officer and I am passionate about bringing change into society. I know, people say this all the time but my body, heart, and soul owes a lot to my nation" says Aksha, 16- year-old girl who has initiated a moment amongst her friends which enforces them to stand against littering. Aksha is generally seen carrying her 'D' bag which plays the role of a hanging dustbin. The Girl has already started paying her share of goodness to the nation. Have you?

Story 8

Hot-Blooded Did Cold Callings!

"Me? I was a complete introvert till the time I realized that expression and success are like Brother and Sister. Any amount of knowledge is worthless till the time you are ready to express yourself. I can still recall a day from the past when I tried my hand on online personality test which indicated the reserved nature I had. When I moved to Australia from Punjab (India), I realized that a degree with exceptional grades is not enough for a successful career. I started reading inspirational novels and started attending sessions of booming businessmen. There was one thing which was common amongst all of them, their ideologies were the same. They didn't bother about what others will think of them. They all were open to failures" says Gurpreet Singh, 26-year-old boy with life-changing cold calling experiences. "We accept change in our lives only when a blue day approaches us. I had to earn well in a far off land, so I welcomed all the constraints with open arms. I started working on my communication skills, personality and taught myself the art of initiation. I pushed myself for some random talks with random people. Soon, I was there training others on skill development. It was exactly like a miracle" says an Extroverted Turban Guy.

Young people like me come to Australia and end up driving Taxis. I don't say that it is wrong but I believe that they somehow press down their passion and energy to do big in life. I didn't want myself to compromise on my skills, so I worked on myself, he added.

Story 9

He Direct Those Viral Videos On Internet!

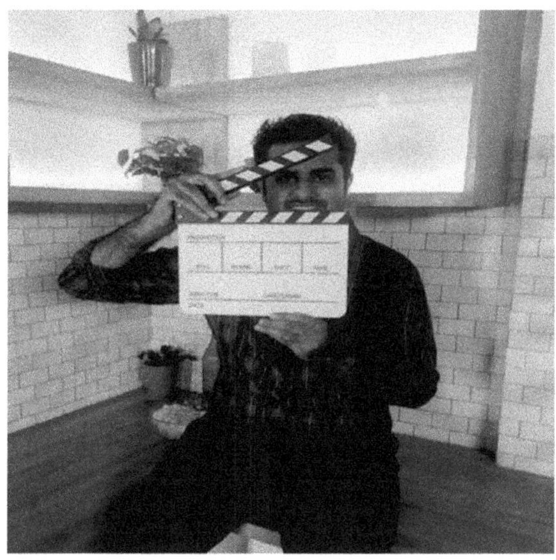

"At his age, I owned a car; I was married, had babies and was completely settled. God knows what he is going to do with his life" someone said this for me 4 years ago. I met the same person a few days back and he was like "Man you are a rising star of our family".

I had an unambiguous aim since I was 12 years old. I knew I would become a Successful Film Director. I started with selling burgers at a shop as a part-time job from 6 pm - 10 pm to earn Rs100 each day. Soon, I got work as an assistant director for just 3 days shoot and I was paid Rs1800. I would envy my friends as they all were earning well and I was almost empty pocket. I have also sold A4 size sheets by visiting offices randomly. I would then sell Books and notebooks in schools as well. My parents were worried and I was frustrated and I would habitually tell lies to people about my job. But, all this time I was upgrading my technical knowledge about the camera and its movements.

29th September 2015 I got a call from one production house and they said that they wanted to meet me. It was my first regular job and I earned Rs 7000 per month. It was the beginning of a new life for me and I never looked back then.

You would be surprised to know that I worked as an Assistant Director during the shoot of film 'Dangal' with 200 advertisement films which are viral on social media these days. My clients include Urbanclap, Dove, Brooke Bond and many more. I am currently working on a Series including Indian Cricketers. Film and Fashion world has become a part of my life now and my salary has no boundaries.

Story 10

I Was Too Stiff To Even Dance!

"During my college days, I took part in a dance show as all my friends were joining the same. The very first day they all sensed that my body was too stiff to dance. I danced like a Robot literally.

College was over and days passed with a very irregular lifestyle. There was no time table for meals, sleep or study. I decided to join a yoga class just to fix the habit of getting up early in the morning. Soon I realized that my health was getting better. The toned boy and stable mind showered bliss upon me the whole day long. I could relate the reason for my cheerful mood to the morning yoga exercises. Yoga became a part of my life. One day someone said to me that 'MY BODY was too flexible and apt for movements'. Really? I couldn't believe the transformation which yoga had offered me.

But, like every story, there was a slight curl in mine too. My marriage was approaching and I skipped my morning routine for almost 4 months. I craved to practice yoga again. I couldn't resist myself so I joined some advanced classes again. Every day there is 1 hour which I keep at bay for

Yoga is 'MY Time' and that is the best part of my day. I think it gives me a positive aura which keeps my soul, body, and mind at peace.

Story 11

Lean To Let Go!

"I was a Graphic designer and I have done that sitting job for a good 6 years. I would keep my juggling balls on my table while working on the computer just to keep myself motivated. After working for around 20 -30 minutes, I would take some rejuvenating break and juggle them. This kept me lively and relaxed. I soon discovered that I was hurting every inch of my body by continuously sitting in the same posture for hours.

Notwithstanding that designing was creative, it became a drag for me. All this started tossing my mind when I joined a community to learn Slacklining. Slackline is an art to balance your body by trusting your soul and concentrating your mind. I have always liked the idea of challenging myself with different tasks and in this way, I have learned many different ways for body control, coordination, trust, strength, flexibility and most importantly letting go in the form of Acro Yoga.

I am always on a move to different places in search of more knowledge to gain and share. I wish everyone starts paying attention to their body, mind, and soul as early as possible in their lives" says Arunesh Moudgil whose appearance might have grabbed you just the way it attracted us too.

Story 12

If Your Baby Is Hyper-Active, It's A Blessing!

"Everyone took their steps back whenever I enrolled her to some academy. She was a hyper-active child and it would become too difficult for the tutors to teach her anything. I knew that she possessed unimaginable amount of energy in herself and it would sometimes become too exhausting to control her. But, I didn't leave hope. I decided to channelize her energy in a manner which can act as a blessing for her. I quit my job and decided to work on my child whom I knew was a blessing and not a curse. Today my 8-year old daughter Hiya is a National Level recognized Dance champion and she practices over 8 hours each day. That is the sum of energy I was talking about!" says Meeta Nanda who has lately started her own venture to train kids on various grounds. Hiya has a keen interest in Chess which helps her to build her concentration which usually lacks in the hyper-active kids, shared Meeta.

We had a small chit chat with Hiya as well and she was all gaga over the fact that her story is going to be uploaded soon. She in her virtuous voice said "I want to be the world's best dancer and I will keep on devoting my time to my passion. I am also learning Hula Hoop and I study everyday to maintain pace with my academics as well. Mumma doesn't allow me much breaks between the practice sessions and I assure her to Dance without a halt".

The only Mantra which this Mother-daughter follows is "Universe loves the stubborn heart". The results are right there in front of you!

Story 13

10 Years Ago He Was A Sweeper!

"It was a Love Marriage and I had no job so whatever came across me, I said yes! Fortunately or unfortunately I was offered the job of a sweeper at a hospital while I was 27 years old. Soon, I joined a part-time job as a utensil cleaner at a hotel which sustained my family. I never could have imagined that perhaps after 10 years I will become a fill fledged counselor at the same hospital. You have read it right. My journey was not too difficult as I was always keen on learning new things which helped me step on the ladder to success. Even though my qualifications were restricted to 12th grade, I learned computers, dealing with people, learned counseling art and was the one who got an authentic training on the same. I helped the front desk people for making slips for the patients; I would replace someone at the operation theatre in their absence and would always be ready to put myself in situations which can teach me new lessons. I am now a Medical eye counselor and earning 30 times higher than what I used to earn back then as a sweeper. My father-in- law doesn't dislike me now!" Sublin Kumar, 41- year-old who is also the Chairman of Anti Corruption Cell of his District.

Story 14

My Journey Is Captured!

"I didn't know how to hold a mic even, yet I always wanted to hold one. It was just a dream which I thought can never be achieved. I was a Technical Student and Entertainment Industry was not something which I felt can ever accept me. I was somehow determined to do something unique with my life. As I was always fond of Public speaking so I took a chance by sitting for an interview which demanded a good voice over artist. I kept it a secret for my Family. I was selected for the profile and gradually they offered me to interview Bollywood and Pollywood Celebrities, Business Women and many esteemed personalities. Every day, I read Punjabi books to advance my communication skills. I now research a lot before taking someone's interview and sit at Big Press Conferences with other Journalist friends. With no degree in Journalism, I am still called as a Journalist" says Raman, a celebrity anchor and a girl full of passion.

Phalak Betab

Story 15

Find Your Thing!

"While I was in my 3rd grade, there was something like a blackout in the city on the very same day when I had a stage performance in my school. My teachers decided to wind it up but I didn't leave a stone unturned to convince them that the performance would take place, no matter what!" shared the girl who has made a debut in Punjabi industry with the recently released Punjabi Song with renowned Actor "I always wanted to be an actress and I knew that I was made for this. The corporate job, which I did for 9 months, was like an endless ride which reiterated me with the fact that I was born to ACT, and ACT, and ACT. 3 years back I took admission in School of Communication studies, Panjab University to follow my passion. My teachers from the past funded me for the same, not because I was financially weak but because I kept it as a disclosed decision from my parents. The day when I got the opportunity to interview Gulzaar Sahib, my father sensed my passion and realized that I could do something with my life" says Soumya Joshi who believes that Indian families are conditioned in a manner which ignites fear in them to not let their children become Artists for the obvious reasons.

"All these years, since 2003 I was always doing theatre without looking for any sort of recognition and that kept my skills alive. The day I got a call for my selection for a Punjabi MovieI was ecstatic as finally, I had done something to make my Grandfather (Nana Papa) proud. He was after all my support system throughout the journey of my life. One day while I was shooting on the set, the news of his demise reached me. I could have easily left the spot but I was his pride, he always wanted me to follow my heart. So, I decided to shot the scene which demanded me to laugh out loud or you may call it LOL. That day was a real beginning!"

I suggest each one of you, sit quietly and ponder on Finding Your thing, Your passion! .

Story 16

Preparing For Government Exam?

"While I was practicing Nursing, I realized that there were many instances where I was not permitted to take the decisions. People who are doing serving jobs can completely understand the steps you need to cross, to reach the decision making authority. The long process usually dilutes the purpose. I decided to prepare myself for the civil services examination. The decision was taken with an open mind and heart and I knew that hurdles will surely come my way. I didn't pay much heed to those problems which, I knew, were meant to come my way. I started studying with the will to learn something new each day. It was not at all a pain for me; I was savoring the enlightenment, which was showering wisdom on me. Boom and Busts are part of a journey and I believe that we should not cling onto anything. Also, everyone's journey is different and unique, so is their solutions!" says Assistant Commissioner of Income Tax Jyotinder Kaur Bajwa.

Phalak Betab

Story 17

Plights Are Here Forever, Don't Let Them Overpower You!

"When he turned 7, I had tried every possible way to take him out of the difficulties he was facing. My son was as capable as other children except for the fact that he had issues while connecting socially. I knew the fact that he had a rare Asperger syndrome, a condition which affects the ability to effectively socialize and communicate. However, the social set-up at that time was not supportive and people would ignore talking about the same. There was a scarcity of information available on the internet. My entire life had changed while I was just 27 years old and would sometimes hold myself responsible for not being careful enough during the pregnancy days. The bewildered thoughts made me vulnerable to paralytic stroke as well. But, somewhere deep inside I was sure that I was strong enough to deal with the situation"says Sharmita Bhinder, who is a core believer of unmasking the realities of humankind.

"I was always keen to work for social welfare and there I was held in a situation where partaking towards the same became a reason for me to live. I came up with an NGO named 'Empower' with an aim to take out such parents and children from the cocoon and discuss. Gradually, people started joining us and Music, dance, and other Art forms became a therapy for the children. My Baby is now a theatre artist, fashion show star and has so many accolades in his name. I am proud of my son, Manav and all those children who are special in their own way" she added Sharmita Bhinder.

Story 18

Couple Who Serves Together, Stays Together!

I would often grab a bite from this eating joint which is run by an elderly couple at the University Campus. Years passed on, students kept on changing, but the couple remained there serving brunches to everyone. One day, when I visited them randomly, I thought of knowing their story and they were happy to share the same. The story goes on like this....

"I was practicing as an Advocate for good 15+ years and sitting next to me is my wife who was a highly qualified teacher. The days were passing by smoothly till the time we realized that our sons were turning young. One of them is currently in America and another one in an IIT.

We didn't want to stop them from exploring their potentials as that would cost them leaving their dreams and sticking to us. Thus, we decided to leave our jobs and find a way to stay with EACH OTHER" said Ashutosh Sharma who has been operating this eating joint from past 10 years along with his wife, Rajni Sharma, at Panjab University. "There can't be any better work than this as it allows us to stay together for the whole day. Our love is growing, and so is our understanding" says Rajni.

Story 19

Even Though Camera Was Not My Dream, It Is Now An Achievement!

"It was never a passion for me; I was just learning photography because my friend was doing the same. I was around 17 when I started working at a vegetable outlet, as we were not financially sound; the owner of the shop was a part-time photographer. We used to sell vegetables along with learning the skill to click. Soon, I was interning under a Mentor who was a professional in clicking the pictures of dead bodies and inside scenario of operation theatres.

It was a little bizarre, but he ultimately taught me the basics. Soon, I grasped interest in it as people started praising me a lot. I would always starve for positive feedbacks rather than money. I have no academic qualification; whatever I have learned is all by myself. I would organize my shoots alone and then with the hit-and-trial method would come up with new tricks, which were not in the books even! Name a celebrity and I have done a photoshoot with him/her! It feels great, as all this while, I have been able to give a comfortable life to my single-parent, my Mother!" shared Dheeraj Mourya, a renowned freelance photographer. The boy says that his quest for knowledge is not going to stop anytime soon. In the world, where everyone is a Photographer, he is a little unique and sassy.

Story 20

Hoops Have Encircled Me For Life!

"I was 13 years young when I first tried Hula Hooping during a school activity. At that time I didn't imagine that these hoops will encircle me later in life & become my profession. Hoops kept coming back to me time and again at different points during my journey. Hula hooping turned out to be a hobby for me till I gradually realized that I craved to explore it further, keeping aside my degree in fashion design, a 9-5 design job & career as a dancer/freelancer. Also with hardly any Indians exploring this field, it was even more challenging for me to take it up & explore it further.

My dad having served the Indian embassy at a foreign lands possibly had different ideas of what I'd chose as a career, but I chose to follow my own path, which he gradually accepted even though hesitant at first. I made the best use of the public workout areas in Korea where hoops were kept for people to use. All of my hard work over the years paid as I got associated with platforms likeDance India Dance,Kingdom of Dreams, India Banega Manch , Decathlon, and so many more. Hooping surely is meant for all body types contrary to the misconception that it is for kids alone. I believe that hooping is a good way to stay fit & active, but at the same time we must not forget that fitness is so personal. I cannot think of generalizing it with a fixed routine plan for everyone or encompass it into a fixed plan to hoop to lose weight.

This wasn't my purpose of hooping. For me it was more for the performing art aspect of it. I usually get asked as to how many hoops I can hoop with at a time to which I'd say that for me hooping is a balance between the creative ways in which a single hoop can be manipulated in movement, to exploring double hooping, & also challenging myself with the different elements I can perform by adding the number of hoops each time. My journey was not as simple as it seems to be. Being rejected from countless design job interviews & shows taught me to move ahead and keep working nevertheless" says Rajni Ramachandran, India's well-known Hula Hoop artist.

Story 21

When You Help Someone, You Enrich Yourself!

"I always fantasized a Government Job which could offer me a lavish Car embellished with red beacons atop it. My teacher once told me, 'You are a hardworking boy and diligence never go waste'; I have kept his teachings alive within me till today. With consistent efforts and a focused mind I once received Gold Medal from Nobel Laureate, Abdus Salam; this achievement could not have been possible if I would have not got inspired from my sister who received a Gold Medal from the Governor. Coming back to my dream of becoming a Government official, I became an Assistant Planner and was posted to Varanasi.

Even though the red beacon was there but my near and dear ones were not there to see and celebrate it with me. Soon, riots hovered the city because of Indira Gandhi's assassination and I had no option but to leave my dream job and come back to my state Punjab. I had already experienced life at its worst during that phase when I was struggling to survive as the movement against the Sikh community horrified me. I later joined Guru Ram Das school of planning, Guru Nanak Dev

University, Amritsar and realized that the best job in the whole world is a Job which lets you share your knowledge with others." After serving there as a Professor and Head, he joined as an advisor Amritsar, Smart City.

With 3 Master Degrees in hand; Sociology, Town Planning and Architectural Conservation, Dr. Balvinder Singh is the 1st Turban Sikh to get a scholarship in the University of York for pursuing his Masters of Architectural Conservation. Having been traveled to 22 countries and winning 18 Awards, he is about to release his book on Historic Sikh Shrines in India and Pakistan. "As I have a passion of clicking pictures so my book will contain pictures that I have clicked myself."

Story 22

Find A Comfortable Spot At The Edge Of Your Seat And Experience The Magic!

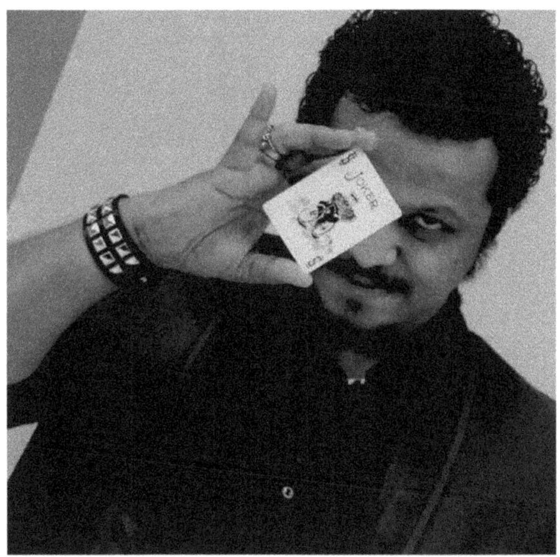

"Every story has a beginning and an ending but magic lovers don't have a story, they only have magic to share! I met one such Magician sitting on the road-side pavement and alluring the passersby with some card tricks. I am talking about that phase of my life when I was an 8th grade kid with a wired passion, I was the type who would come back from lunch break with a frog in his pocket . I would save my lunch money to learn the magic skill from him and would skip my classroom school lectures. His fees kept on escalating and my appetite kept on shrinking. At home, I would lock myself into the bathroom to practice it in front of the mirror.

The results were finally out, and I had flunked my 11th grade. Soon I realized that even though, the new Alma Mater was not as glittery as the previous one but it opened gates for me and changed my life. With the kind support of my new Principal, I got nominated for the 'Student of the year' award led by a leading newspaper, Times of India. A new market opened up for me and there I was performing at Schools, in the morning, and working at a call centre in the afternoon for a livelihood. In 2010, stepping up a ladder, I was nominated for 'India's Top 10 Young Magicians' and was featured on Star 'One's India's Magic Star'.

The trail that followed included Sony Tv's 'Entertainment K Liye, Kuch bhi Karega' and Zee Telegu's 'Big Celebrity Challenge' and have performed for the royal family of Bhutan and at the Taste of India festival in Bahrain besides a host of international shows, says 31 year old, Amazing David, a professional Illusionist or a Modern day Magician.

"I have now come up with a pan-India network (The Konjurors) that creates platforms for upcoming magicians to hone their skills and display their talents"

By the way, Did you listen to his TEDx talk?

Story 23

How This 20-Year Old Bought A House!

"I aspire to become a psychologist. I work 8 hours a day to earn money so that I can finance my education" says Rana Joy Das, 20, from West Bengal who is currently in his final year of graduation and brews coffee at CCD. "My job keeps my mind active and act as a source of self motivation. I am doing it because it is the road to achieve my goals". When we asked him about his daily schedule his answer was swift and clear, "Earlier I used to wake up at 6 in the morning but from the time I have started my job, I choose to wake up at 3 (midnight) so that I can cope up with the studies as well. My constant effort has paid me reward and now I am able to aid my family. Earlier we used to dwell in a rented apartment. We have recently bought our small house now"

Story 24

I Am A Khan From Afghan!

The Arabic word 'Jihad' means a struggle against one's ego & evil inclinations for uplifting social and personal life. The usage of this particular word by the terrorist groups has resulted in Jihad becoming a negative connotation. This was made clear to me by Humayun Khan, the21-year-old native of Afghanistan who is currently pursuing his higher education in India. During a discursive discussion with Humayun, I came across the ground reality of Terrorism.

In his rigid voice, he said, "Terrorism has no religion, but it does have an origin".

This was a direct indication to his neighbouring country Pakistan which he thinks is nurturing the terrible terrorist groups. He shared his firm belief in the fact that terrorism is a result of political agendas hovering over a country which limit its development. "You can't compare Afghanistan and India as of now but I assure you that soon this will happen".

I asked him the reason for his interest in India and like his Indian fellows he too has always been a fond lover of Indian Bollywood and Cricket. "I have been following Akshay Kumar since childhood and that is something which propagated me to choose India for my studies".

After completing his school education at Afghanistan, Humayun opted to study in India, unlike his father who still continues to do research work in America. Not to forget to mention that his father is a political adviser to the president of his country. Belonging to a family background with much wisdom Humayun's future plan involves moving to Europe after completing his Masters in Business Administration from India.

The reason that he shared for not residing in his home country is his quest to gain knowledge from across the globe and finally being able to implement the intellect for the betterment of his country. He wishes to bring swift development to his nation. Do we have such youngsters in India as well? I was stunned to hear nationalistic views from a 21-year-old.

"I am doing all this for Afghanistan and I love my country more than anything else". This doesn't mean that I am unaffected by the terror attacks taking place in other parts of the world. The deadliest Pulwama attack in India, Christchurch city of New Zealand and Easter attack in Sri Lanka has shaken me as much as it did to the citizens of that particular country, he added.

"Afghanistan is far safer than Pakistan and we have a lot of Indian brothers working over there," said Humayun.

"From past 50 years we, Afghans are the biggest sufferers of Terrorism but I can assure you that Islam has nothing to do with it" claimed Humayun with sparkling eyes. The literal meaning of Islam is peace and there are a lot of hindrances mentioned in Quran for any kind of violence, he

Story 25

Story Of The Author

"I was always keen on meeting new people, talking to them and learning something out of it. One day I made up my mind to pen down all the stories that I came across. This book is the result of just a single thought of mine. It is as simple as that! If you have an idea in your mind, make it visible, bring it to actions and the universe is there to support you. This book is a proof of that."

"I will be definitely sharing the stories from my own life in my next book. "

Phalak Betab

www.ingramcontent.com/pod-product-compliance
Lightning Source LLC
LaVergne TN
LVHW051107180726
843512LV00020B/1645